Faith and Culture in Catholic Education

A Guide for Catholic and Non-Catholic Parents

Frank DeSiano, CSP

PAULIST PRESS
New York/Mahwah, NJ

Imprimatur: + Cardinal Edwin F. O'Brien
            Archbishop of Baltimore
            January 25, 2012

Cover design by Lynn Else

Library of Congress Control Number: 2012934105

Published by Paulist Press
997 Macarthur Boulevard
Mahwah, New Jersey 07430
www.paulistpress.com

Printed and bound in the
United States of America

ISBN: 978-0-8091-4782-3

Contents

Foreword

Some of life's most blessed moments are centered around children. Little can compare to the moment when we discover that a woman is with child or our utter joy at the birth of a child. We mark each step along the way as a "first." And, yes, there comes that time when we discern where our children will go to school and deep down we want nothing but the best for them as they grow and mature in life with us at their sides. Enrolling your child in a Catholic school or a parish formation program can be a unique first as well.

There is always the opportunity to send our children to public school, of course. However, there are also other choices that we can make in this regard. I remember when my family moved from New York City to Long Island. In the city, I was in the parish Catholic school. When we moved to the Island, there was no room for us in the Catholic school and public school was the only option at the time. Things were also different when I was a child. Most if not all the children in the Catholic school were Catholic, as were the teachers and the parents who sent them to the school. However, times and demographics have changed.

Today the Catholic Church is trying to counter contemporary economic challenges and see that our schools and religious education programs thrive, not just survive. This is most necessary in our cities. In many ways for us, the Church is making a great investment of her resources to provide the best Catholic education and formation possible for our children whether they are Catholic or not. However, our schools and formation programs also must re-awaken in Catholics a sense of a new evangelization.

Catholic schools and formation programs offer the Church a unique opportunity to share with parents what we believe. We encounter families where one parent is Catholic and the other is not; families where both parents are Catholic; and single parents. Each family has the best interests of the child at heart. Our schools and formation programs exist to form disciples in the challenging times in which we find ourselves. This can be somewhat countercultural in our increasingly secular era, when being religious is not necessarily politically correct. However, Pope Benedict states that we cannot take faith for granted. He challenges Catholic leaders to look at our structures in "Re-proposing faith in a culture which has lost the instinct to believe." Our Catholic institutions began in faith and continue in faith. If those institutions thrive, it is because of the faith of their people.

The Church is creating a culture of formation in our schools and formation programs. This culture consists of:

Recognizing Mission, Call and Need—Catholic education and formation is rooted and enriched by

Christ's great commission to "Go and Make Disciples." This is the simple framework for our mission, our institutions, and all of the Church's ministries and outreach. Jesus calls all believers who have responded to the call to seize all opportunities to spread the Gospel, the Good News of the Risen Lord. In many situations, we find ourselves among those who are not Catholic or who are not practicing their faith. This often happens through the works of Catholic Charities, social justice ministry and yes, Catholic Schools and formation programs. Catholic education and formation involves parents as well as their children. In more and more of these instances, one parent or another is not Catholic or practicing their faith. This book is a great "new" beginning for any parents who avail themselves and their child of Catholic education and formation.

Respecting and Celebrating a Multicultural Church— The Church is and has always been a multicultural place for believers and non-believers. For some, this is a new experience and for others it is a longtime blessing. Catholic education and formation embraces this reality and invites teachers, children, and parents to experience the richness of God's diverse gifts. Readers should approach this book from their own unique cultural perspectives and hopefully each will experience a yearning for what only the Divine can offer.

Acknowledging the Value of Lay Ministry—Today Catholic education and formation would not be possible if it were not for the time and talent of our great lay teachers and formators. This exemplifies the great call of discipleship. Catholic lay men and women are challenged to be working side by side in the mission of the Church. In many instances non-Catholics are invited to share unique gifts which enhance the Catholic culture in the Church's institutions ministries and programs.

Calling for Competency and On-Going Formation— You know full well that you want your children's teachers to be the best. This happens all across the board in ongoing professional development in our Catholic schools and formation programs. Catholic dioceses are making great strides to keep education and formation programs at a high level of quality and providing the excellence that parents expect. However, this competency and ongoing formation is not just for the teachers. It must also include parents. Involvement of the parents in the education and formation of their children is essential.

Providing for Formation and Celebration—In our Catholic schools and formation programs, Catholic children also experience the fullness of initiation in the Church through special celebrations in the sacramental life. However, all children, including those who are not Catholic, can benefit from this element of Catholic education, which will help form them into mature human beings, created in the image and likeness of God.

Establishing Clear Expectations—It is important for everyone involved in Catholic schools and formation programs to understand that there are expectations of parents that are essential for the sake of a good education and formation. The co-responsibility between parents and those entrusted with their child's education and formation is critical to the success of the culture that our programs embody. Our children need the support of family and educators to ensure that they get the best that Catholic education and formation has to offer. For parents of Catholic children this is extremely critical, especially when children are being prepared for the Sacraments.

Serving as Role Models and Collaborators—Parents are the first people that children look up to as role models. And their teachers are next. This unique bond between parents and teachers can enable a collaboration that is unique and can last a lifetime. This dual relationship in Catholic education is essential in order for students to benefit from all that the Catholic Church has to offer in its education and formation programs.

In this book, Father DeSiano provides important advice and support for those who have chosen to enroll their children in a Catholic school.

Rev. John E. Hurley, CSP, DMin.

Paulist Father John Hurley currently serves as the founding Executive Director of the Department of Evangelization for the Archdiocese of Baltimore. He also served as the Executive Director of the United States Conference of Catholic Bishops Secretariat for Evangelization and the National Pastoral Life Center.

Introduction
John E. Hurley, CSP

The Department of Evangelization in the Archdiocese of Baltimore began a *New Evangelization* initiative to reach out to all parents of children in Catholic education and formation. Paulist Father Frank DeSiano joined this project and was asked to be a part of the department's listening groups, made up of individuals that this book reaches out to. Father DeSiano wrote the principle text for this book and collaborated with members of the department to finalize the text. The department wishes to express its gratitude to Father. DeSiano who seized this opportunity to reach out to people we encounter every day in varying relationships with the Church.

This book is designed for three types of constituencies: **Catholic diocesan leaders**, **faith formators** in our schools and parishes, and **parents**.

To Catholic Diocesan Leaders:

Bishops, superintendants of Catholic schools and directors of faith formation have a new unique tool to place in the hands of Catholic and non-Catholic parents alike in orientation programs. In our Catholic schools and formation programs we encounter parents whose relationships with the Church are varied, as well as those with no relationship to the Church.

> In our Catholic schools, we find Catholic parents who are very engaged in the life and activity of the Church. We find families with both a Catholic and a non-Catholic parent. And we find families where both parents are non-Catholics. All parents, however, want to provide the best education and formation possible.

> In our Catholic formation programs, we find Catholic parents who are very engaged in the life and activity of the Church, as well as Catholic parents who are not engaged. We find families with both a Catholic and a non-Catholic parent, both of whom want their children to experience the sacramental life of the Church.

In a culture where faith is becoming more and more nominal, it is important for Church leaders to seize every opportunity to invite Catholic parents to be more deeply involved in the faith formation of their children. This book provides a unique opportunity for you, in your leadership roles, to respond optimally to Pope Benedict's call for a *New Evangelization*.

Catholic schools and formation programs offer a unique opportunity for leaders to meet parents where they are and invite them into a deeper relationship with their children's education and formation. **This book is an excellent tool to be included in your orientation**

material for parents who are enrolling their child in a Catholic school or in a Catholic formation program.

It provides a good foundation to better understand and appreciate the culture of Catholic education and formation and to maximize the opportunities presented throughout the year.

It helps **Catholic parents** to appreciate better the unique opportunities they have to share in their child's education to be co-responsible in the sacramental formation of their child.

It helps **non-Catholic parents** to appreciate better the unique opportunities they have to share in their child's education. It explains why their children, though they may not be able to participate in the Church's sacraments, will nevertheless come to a better appreciation of what these sacraments mean in the Catholic Church.

Father DeSiano outlines the unique opportunities for parents to be co-responsible with the teachers in the education and formation of their child.

To Pastors, Principals, Parish Catechetical Leaders, and Faith Formators:

Your commitment to providing quality faith formation for our children is only enhanced by outreach to parents. This book will enable you to accomplish the following.

Facilitate small group discussion by having parents discuss the content of the book or the "points to ponder" at the end of each session.

Provide parents with reading material that will enable them to understand better the faith their child is being exposed to.

Provide answers for a generation of parents that is searching for meaning, and raise thought-provoking new questions that invite deeper reflection and that might lead to surprising blessings.

Inspire us to ask, each step of the way, what we are doing what we are doing to promote Catholic identity.

To Parents:

The Church believes that you have made a good decision to enroll your child in a Catholic school or a parish formation program and understands that there is considerable sacrifice involved in this decision. There is the financial sacrifice, of course. In faith formation programs, there are also the challenges of balancing time commitments and keeping faith formation as a priority in your child's life. Whether your child is in a Catholic school or a parish faith formation program, the Church is also making a significant commitment to you. The Church does so because she believes in what she is doing.

As the doors of faith are opened to their children, Catholic parents have a unique opportunity to reassess their own faith life. How can I as a parent support my child and be a good role model in faith?

Non-Catholic parents who send their child to Catholic school will hopefully come to a greater understanding of why Catholic education is such a priority today. Something has led you to this choice, and in time, you will more deeply appreciate its significance for both you and your child. In addition, even though your child may not be able to participate in the sacraments, your child and you will come to an understanding of the core elements of our Catholic faith and the richness of our tradition.

As you read this book, you will have opportunities to re-examine all the motivations you may have had in choosing Catholic education and formation for your children. Hopefully all your expectations will be fulfilled in this collaborative process. You now have a unique opportunity to be co-responsible with teachers in enabling your child to fully develop all of his or her God-given talents. And it is our hope that as the years unfold you will come to a deeper understanding of why we do what we do in Catholic education and formation. Some of the answers are in this book. If you have other questions, there are people on your campus who are more than willing to sit down with you and explain the Catholic faith. Don't be shy. If you have questions, always ask! You have placed your trust in the Church, and she in turn is committed to the spiritual and academic development of your loved ones.

Welcome!

T hank you for bringing your child to us. This short book will help orient you to the Catholic community, particularly with reference to the ways we can serve your child and your family.

It has five parts:

> **Part 1** will invite you to reflect on what it is you really want for your child, your family and yourself.

> **Part 2** will give you a sense of what the Catholic Church has to offer you.

> **Part 3** will give you some tips on feeling at home with us Catholic people.

> **Part 4** asks you to reflect where God might be leading you in your life.

> **Part 5** provides a short overview of "Things Catholic" that you might want to know about.

The purpose of this book is to make your interaction with the Catholic Church easier and clearer. People can have many anxieties about their family, particularly around what is best for their children. They may have varying degrees of familiarity with the Catholic Church and its main directions—ranging from a lot of knowledge to very little. This book provides an easy way to find out some basic things and organize any questions or issues you might have.

We pray that God, who has blessed you and your family, will bestow ever more blessings on you as you partner with us in providing what is best for your child.

One

What Are You Asking For?

Nothing forces us back to basics like children do. We marvel at their births. We wonder as they grow. We see them as creation itself come alive, right before our eyes.

As we have grown through the years, we've made adjustments in our own lives—compromises that perhaps we are unwilling to make in the lives of our children. We have made our accommodations and slowly begin to limit our hopes. Whatever wild dreams we might have once had, whatever fantasies about our future, we think we know our limitations now, the scope of what's possible for us. We've made our truce.

But when it comes to our children—that's something else.

They represent so much potential, so much unfulfilled dreaming, so much openness, and such a range of possibility—and we shudder at the thought that any of this possibility might be cut short or remain incomplete.

So a child—my child or any child—represents totally open dreams.

1

Just as we would do anything at all for them, so we expect life to open itself richly, and without reserve, for them.

So what are the basics? What is the DNA of our human dreams? What are our hopes for our children?

It's probably not easy to be specific because our dreams, in today's climate, are so wrapped up with cultural expectations. Surely our child will graduate from grade school and high school—and surely college as well. Our child will have a great career, marry well, have sufficient money and lots of love. Our child will live to be old, so old that she or he will live long enough to see death as a relief. Our child will be surrounded by children and grandchildren, content with what has been achieved.

These are, after all, the dreams we have for ourselves, dreams that come partly true in most modern lives. We do live longer than earlier generations, with more modern conveniences, with more options, than most people in the past could ever have had. We have fallen in love, have generally healthy lives, and hope to forestall the grim reaper enough to make it well into our eighties. Of course, as we get older, we wonder if our lives could have been richer, if we made the right choices, if we shaped our possibilities as well as we could have.

However we feel about our lives, we wish for our children the ideals that have rewarded us—we wish them this—and even more.

But what is the "more" that we wish them?

What is the "more" we wish we had, even for ourselves?

What We Seek

Perhaps that's why you have brought your child into this encounter with the Catholic Church. Perhaps you see in us something of the fullness you wish for your child and, indeed, for yourself.

For how many centuries has the Catholic community formed children on many levels? In one sense, the whole process of educating children as a way to better their lives, and open those lives up to all of life's riches, was developed by the Catholic Church—the whole insistence that education and formation brought people fuller lives.

It might be Catholic school education.

It might be faith formation outside a Catholic school.

It might be the breadth of Catholic culture as children connected to each other and their wider society through music, athletics, social service and religious expression.

It might be to request the sacrament of Baptism.

However it has been expressed in our Catholic history, it has always meant more than just getting ahead, just getting an education, just receiving the sacraments.

People bring their children to the Catholic Church because of the way the dreams of God become intertwined with our human hopes. The Catholic Church offers a vision of life, one in which God takes our human aspirations—our deepest human hopes—and puts them into the vision of universal love and universal life.

Thank You

So we are grateful you have brought your child to us. We are grateful for the opportunity we have to serve your child and you. And we are grateful for the trust you place in us.

Your coming to us says, in some way, how much you implicitly see the Catholic vision as part of your life—and, more importantly, your child's life. It says that the two-thousand years of witness and life which compose our Catholic experience is important to you. It says that you want some of this Catholic experience for your child, for what is most precious and important in your own life.

We are deeply honored by your trust.

In response to it, we pledge to cherish your child with the very love of God.

We know that family relationships can be complicated in today's world. The romantic *Leave It to Beaver* or *Cosby Show* image of family life usually doesn't reflect the way things actually are. In many families, there are different religious traditions, and occasionally conflicts arise among family members because of this. Still other families are torn apart by separation or divorce. Sometimes grandparents have to undertake the religious training, and even the whole education, of a child. Almost all families have unending schedules for their children—schedules filled with opportunities that sometimes even compete with religious training.

Because we serve so many families, we know how difficult family life can be today.

So, thank you for coming to us.
We are privileged to serve you and your child.

Hopes

So what do you want for your child?

There are many reasons parents bring their children to us. Some people want the safe environment we provide, others know that the Church provides a better education than they might receive elsewhere. Still others come honoring a faith commitment made to a spouse; a promise to raise their child in the Catholic faith. But all parents come to the Catholic Church knowing we will provide values for their children.

We have come to see most of these values as basically *human* values. Honesty, integrity, sincere application of one's efforts, the ability to relate well with others, concern for people around us—these kinds of values are represented in almost all world religions.

We call this the "Golden Rule": to treat others as you yourself wish to be treated, to not do anything to another person that we would not want done to ourselves.

Whatever commentators say about modern attitudes, most people subscribe to a basic decency which they expect from others. That decency at the least involves a negative: to refrain from anything that hurts or diminishes another.

But it also can be put in a positive light: to do to others all the good that can be done. To live so as to enhance the lives of others and, in a sense, all humankind.

Once our hopes start down this road, however, we begin to open up a whole other level of hope, a whole other kind of dreaming. We begin to grapple with basic notions of what human life is all about, the inherent value of every human being, and how life's meaning implies a set of values that go beyond the minimum we need to survive.

If we are "products of evolution," as some might put it, we are indeed marvelous products, with minds that range the entire universe, and hearts that extend to everything and everyone. If love brings life to fullness, then the greatest love—love for and between everyone—would be our greatest fulfillment. Thoughts like this hover at the edges of our hopes, our dreams.

They also tell us the value of every person because all deserve, at a basic level, love. The existence of every child, loved instinctually by parents, tells us this. If every human being has inherent value, that value must come from the source of reality itself. It has to come before we exist, and it has to extend to all existence.

Most people call this source of reality "God," although some religious traditions may stop short of saying this.

Our hopes inevitably involve unending hopes, irrepressible desires for the deepest, the fullest, the most alive, the most loving. Our hopes for our children involve the One who brings our children wondrously into existence, the One who promises all humans who open their hearts the fullness of life.

So beyond simply human values, we look for a deeper set of values, ones that bring our children into relationship with God and with God's revelation. More than simply being decent, we want our children to thrive, to shine, to express life's wonderful depth. We want them to love all people, but to do this loving with an expansiveness, a generosity, that characterizes the greatest of human beings.

This is another reason you bring your child to the Catholic Church. Every generation of Catholic believers has produced people who exemplify this generosity of love. We all think of St. Francis, who lived in the 1200s; but before and after him, we have countless witnesses to God's love who stopped at nothing to bring that love to the world.

In our own day, the simple woman from Albania who could not let people die abandoned on streets in Calcutta, Mother Theresa, automatically comes to mind.

Maybe you don't think of your child as a saint.

But you undoubtedly would not mind one bit if they walked in the footsteps of outstanding, generous, loving people who have lived their lives in deep relationship with God. In some way, when you bring your child to the Catholic Church, you are looking to help your child become a disciple, a follower of Jesus, one who bears in his or her life the same traits that Jesus showed the world.

Jesus

Jesus is the center of Catholic life. His person, his teaching, and the purpose for which he lived—the Kingdom of God. Jesus gave us a sweeping vision of

God's loving relationship with all people, and the freedom that comes to us when we become conscious of, and live out of, this renewed relationship.

We might hear the word "Kingdom" as if it was some vast political or commercial enterprise. Thousands of years of history condition us to hear it that way. But if we think of "Kingdom" as something like an "environment" we will start to get the correct image. The Kingdom is a whole way existence can be, a dynamic set of relationships. The Kingdom of God does not only come in the future; it begins now, with the way we live. It begins with the hope that we have for a future fuller than the present.

This certainly speaks to the hopes you have for your child. Not only: What kind of world do I want for my child? More importantly: What kind of world will I strive to bring about for the sake of my child, for the sake of all children, for the sake of humankind itself?

So the Kingdom of God touches on the environment you hope to create for your child and for the broader world.

Jesus' life underscores the meaning of the Kingdom.

Jesus lives to show God's mercy and peace, to bring the promise of healing and forgiveness, to expand our narrower mindsets until they reflect the expansiveness of God's love. In situation after situation, Jesus frees people from what traps them, whether illness or social constraints, whether sin or despair: Jesus brings into our world the freedom that comes from the dream God has for us.

Jesus' focus is for those at the bottom, those whom religious leaders and society were ignoring or dismissing: the poor, the crippled, the leprous, the more notorious of sinners. Every healing was a promise of universal healing, every liberation a proclamation of universal freedom.

Once people brought to Jesus a woman caught in adultery. They wanted Jesus to approve their stoning of her. As if she was the only sinner! Jesus simply says, "Whoever is without sin, throw the first stone," and starts doodling on the ground. One by one, the accusers walk away, not because the woman did not sin, but because they realized there's plenty of sin to go around, even among the righteous. "No one is here to condemn you," says Jesus when he notices the crowd has disappeared. "Neither will I. Go and sin no more" (John 7:1–10).

We can feel the drama Jesus brought to situations like this, especially when he confronts those who resented the very help and healing he brought. It's a drama of conflict: dreams versus the humdrum; hope versus a comfortable cynicism.

This conflict grows until, at the death of Jesus, we see it as the ultimate conflict between an unlimited goodness and a darkened vision. For proclaiming the Kingdom, for showing us God's dream, for expanding our narrow human hearts, Jesus becomes a victim, a victim on behalf of all of us. In his suffering, he bears all suffering. In his death, he reveals the brokenness of every death. In his passion, he reveals both the ugly, vast, extent of sin—and also sin's ultimate powerlessness.

Catholics, like all Christians, believe that Jesus was raised from the dead as the Father's definitive judgment over sin and death. In Jesus' resurrection, God offers hope, peace, forgiveness and life to all people who are open to the Kingdom. Some people, to be sure, live for the Kingdom without even recognizing it. But to those who recognize and accept the Kingdom, to those who receive the Spirit of Christ in faith, the realm of God becomes clear, the world begins to shine with God's grace.

This is the world that Catholic life, formation, and education wants to open for every child who comes to us—to place the very mind of Jesus Christ into the mentality of every child, so that we may live as Jesus lived, judge as Jesus judged, serve as Jesus served, and love as Jesus loved.

We cannot think of a greater goal than this for your child—and for your family.

The Catholic community rejoices to be involved with you in creating this new, better world for your child. We appreciate your trust and your coming to us so very much.

Of course, this goal encompasses all the other goals we may seek for our children—personal, moral, physical, and intellectual growth. Society universally applauds our Catholic tradition of education and formation because it acknowledges the numbers of Catholics who advance in education, who seek to serve others, and who contribute in stellar ways to society. Such achievement, laudable as it is, remains only part of what we hope to do. We feel achievement is all the richer as it arises from, and contributes to, an environment of faith.

What Do You Seek?

The birth and growth of your child opens many possibilities—for your child and for you. You come to the Church looking for certain values and goals. May God bless you for the hopes you have for your child.

Our pledge is to further these hopes as much as possible.

But our invitation is for you to revisit your hopes, you deepest—and perhaps hidden—hopes…to be bold and daring because stinginess is not the way God deals with us.

Points to Ponder

1. What are your dreams for your child?

2. How does your affiliation with the Catholic Church help you to realize these dreams?

3. What are some of the questions you have about the Catholic Church?

4. What if any are your concerns about your child's involvement?

Two

What the Catholic Community Can Offer You and Your Family

We have already asked you to reflect on what you might be looking for; we have already thanked you for bringing your child to us, and giving us the privilege to serve you.

Now we would like to sketch briefly some of what the Catholic community can offer you and your family.

With more than a billion believers, a history of two thousand years of witness to Jesus, and a cultural history that can rival any other, the Catholic family of faith has, indeed, a lot to offer. Depending on the needs, desires and receptivity of people who come in contact with us, we can give people so much of what they are looking for.

We recognize that people have a variety of ways of relating to us, some of which may vary quite a bit in terms of intensity. Our commitment is to serve you, where you are, with the concerns you have. Our hope is that, as we serve you, you will also have the chance to deepen your life of faith. If we can accompany you on that deepening, and if we can contribute to it, that will bring all the more joy to us because we will then be fulfilling the commission that Jesus gave to us.

We can briefly sketch what we, as the Catholic people, have been—and strive to be:

A Community

Committed to the furthering of all humankind

In a spirit of openness and love

Through the vision and mission of faith

Communicated by Jesus and his Spirit

Which becomes actualized in the way of life

That we call discipleship

A Community

The Catholic Church can, for sure, seem like a vast and even impersonal organization. How many people think of us primarily as an institution? They enumerate the numbers of buildings and acres of land. They calculate Catholic resources. They ruminate on the various modes of Catholic influence throughout society.

It's all too easy to look at the Catholic Church in cultural stereotypes—the cathedrals, the large complex of buildings, the broad influence on society—and think of it only as a large institution.

Let's face it, in today's society institutions often look unwieldy and self-important. People, since the 1960s in any case, have come to look upon institutions only with suspicion. Indeed, when Catholics were first coming to the United States, we looked like a foreign, international conspiracy; people thought we had a separate government and owed political allegiance to the pope in Rome.

Some of these past images, and many of today's stereotypes, still linger unchallenged.

That is why we would like to give you another image of Catholics: not an "organization" but a community, not an "institution" but a family.

All the possessions and structure of the Catholic Church only go to serve one purpose: to allow people to become a community in a local neighborhood. We call this community a "parish." A parish is not a building or a complex of buildings. It is an assembly, a gathering, a coming together into relationship of people who have bonded with each other.

A parish is a family of families.

Some of our parishes might be quite large—about half our parishes are the size of what we call, in today's terminology, a megachurch (defined as having two thousand members). Many of our parishes are medium-sized or even quite small. But, whatever the size, Catholics connect with other Catholics within the parish, always on the level of respect and caring, but often on the level of friendship. Though we tend not to be clannish (we don't always hang out with our own kind), we do tend to be unpretentious, roll-up-the-sleeves kinds of people who feel deeply connected to each other.

Many of these connections run along peer lines— empty-nesters befriending other empty-nesters, young parents with other parents, parents of teens with parents of other teens, and young adults finding others in their age group. But not always. A family is intergenerational, and so often are the relationships with a parish family. Seniors become involved in service to children; young parents give time to teens or seniors. Young adults become mentors to the generation behind them.

We know some people like to hug, and others feel more comfortable with a bit of distance. Whatever our styles or preferences, the Catholic community can offer you connections, bonds, relationships, which can enrich your life, and the life of your child.

Furthering of Humankind

Catholics, like all Christians, believe in a teaching that changes everything. We believe that the Son of God became became one of us. We call this teaching the "Incarnation," because the word for "flesh" in Latin is *carnis*.

It is a remarkable teaching, one that Christians believe is inescapable given what the Scriptures tell us about Jesus—his deeds, his teaching, his purpose, and his intimate association God the Father. One of the remarkable aspects of this teaching is not only what it says about God; more startling, is what it says about us, about human reality.

This teaching indicates that, in some basic way, human existence has such eminence that it is able to be a vehicle for God. This eminence did not just arise at one moment; rather, all of human experience shares in this exceptional dignity. All of human reality is capable of relating to God. The simple young girl, Mary of

Nazareth, in the quiet of her rural life, opens herself up completely to God as Jesus is conceived within her.

All of humanity, then, has a special dignity. Beyond any divisions into classes, or races, or achievements of talent, every human being is precious in him- or herself before God. No person can claim more than any other person. Every human makes claims by his or her existence.

Of course, we recognize a lot of this in the documents of the United States: "We hold these truths to be self-evident, that all men are created equal...." It took centuries before we could find a civic way to express human dignity; even in America it took a civil war for slaves to be freed and granted status as citizens. And it took a more than a half-century after that before women received a political stature equal to men.

Behind the political ideals lie other ideals, some that come from philosophy, and, in particular, some that come from religion.

St. Mark relates an incident that sheds a lot of light on this. Jesus is teaching in the synagogue and notices a man with a withered hand. He asks: "Is it lawful to do good on the sabbath rather than to do evil, to save life rather than to destroy it?" They had nothing to say to him, the scriptures record; they could not even see the plain logic when it was laid out right before them. St. Mark continues, "[Jesus looked] around at them with anger and grieved at their hardness of heart..." (Mark 3:1–6). As St. Mark sees it, this was the incident that began the political and religious opposition that would lead to the murder of Jesus.

Whatever our religious, philosophical, social, or political categories, the sheer good of humankind has to rank above everything else. Different eras of Christian life have expressed this in different ways. The exorbitant charity that characterized early Christian and Jewish life; the powerful civilizing effect of the monasteries, with monks dedicating themselves not only to scholarship but also to the cultivation of much of the land we call Europe; the gatherings of workers into guilds whose crafts were most powerfully displayed in magnificent cathedrals. As those cathedrals soared, so did the pride of whole cities. "Look at what we accomplished for God!"

Anyone visiting Rome sees displayed, in just about any part of the city, the sculptures and paintings of the Renaissance Church. These were not merely sumptuous artifacts for the sake of church leaders; they were gifts to all the people, all the world, as a legacy of human genius and ideals. The breakdown of illiteracy as society turned more urban and commercial happened with the enormous efforts of priests, religious sisters, and brothers who founded schools for the children of the poor. Hospitals emerged from the works of monasteries, of generous and courageous women, of commitments to care for the sick by believers.

PRINCIPLES OF CATHOLIC
SOCIAL TEACHING

Dignity of the Human Person

All people are sacred, made in the image and likeness of God. People do not lose dignity because of disability, poverty, age, lack of success, or race. The emphasis is on people over things, being over having.

Community and the common good

The human person is both sacred and social. We realize our dignity and rights in relationship with others, in community. As Saint Paul said, "We are one body: when one suffers, we all suffer." We are called to respect all of God's gifts of creation, to be good stewards of the earth and each other.

Rights and responsibilities

People have a fundamental right to life, food, shelter, health care, education, and employment. All people have a right to participate in the decisions that affect their lives.

Corresponding to these rights are duties and responsibilities to respect the rights of others and to work for the common good.

Option for the poor

The moral test of a society is how it treats its most vulnerable members. The poor have the most urgent moral claim on the conscience of any community. We are called to look at public policy decisions in terms of how they affect the poor.

Dignity of work

People have a right to decent and productive work, fair wages, private property, and economic initiative. The economy exists to serve people, not the other way around.

Solidarity

We are one human family. Our responsibilities to each other cross national, racial, economic, and ideological differences. We are called to work globally for justice.

Catholics also recognized how workers were increasingly exploited throughout the nineteenth century. Popes led the way in calling for the dignity of the worker, for just pay for workers, and for the rights of laborers to form unions. This began a rich and lengthy legacy of social teaching, calling for the basic rights of humans to food, shelter, education, and freedom.

Music, art, science, languages, education, health, legal systems to serve justice—you will find the Catholic people right in the middle of all these human advancements.

Because of the humanity of Jesus Christ, human life can never be dismissed.

All of this bears directly upon what the Church can offer you and your child. The cornucopia of human achievement, begotten from the power of Christian faith, lies open for anyone who would reach for its abundant fruits. Every child in our Catholic community can be enriched by the living contact with the enormous human legacy of the Catholic Church.

Sometimes we can get Catholic humanism wrong, as if faith was only concerned with our worldly achievements, as if humanism was the main point. Such an impression would be profoundly wrong. Catholics exalt the human because of humankind's relationship to God—coming from God and heading toward the fullness of God. Catholics affirm human dignity because our relationship with God shows us the breadth and depth of humanity's meaning.

Catholics push forward with human fulfillment because our eyes see the vision of the Kingdom of God. If the Kingdom will come in fullness in the future, that is because the Kingdom is arriving now, in the midst of our human lives.

The dreams you have for your child are one with the dreams of all Catholics and, indeed, of all humankind, for all our children—dreams of our moving forward together into a brighter future, one without war, violence and exploitation, one filled, instead, with love, joy, wisdom, and peace.

Openness and Love

Sociologists distinguish between a cult and a church. A cult is a group that reinforces itself against a wider culture by dynamics that restrict contacts between members and non-members, all buttressed by distinct religious beliefs. A church, on the other hand, sustains a large cultural identity that connects members with the wider world, contributing and receiving a range of perspectives.

With this kind of distinction, the Catholic Church looks like one of the greatest expressions of church in all of history. Although beginning among a group of rural Jews, within one generation it had not only expanded to the major urban centers of the first century—it, even more, began to express itself in the widespread language and ideas of Greek culture. It related to, and absorbed, elements of the cultures of Northern Africa all the way around the Mediterranean to Spain. It focused itself in Rome, then the very center of the ancient world. It expressed itself in an astonishing array of languages. The book of Acts shows this very early in Christian history: "We are Parthians, Medes and Elamites, inhabitants of Mesopotamia, Judea and Cappadocia, Pontus and Asia, Phrygia and Pamphylia, Egypt and the districts of Libya near Cyrene, as well as travelers from Rome..." (Acts 2:9–10). Indeed, Christianity even at this early time touched upon a world of cultures, begetting the "catholic"—universal!—Church.

As a result, being open to culture in all its effects has been a hallmark of Catholic life. Thought and science are among the major effects of culture that the Catholic Church has embraced. The great philosophers of ancient Greece, along with those of the first half-millennium of Christian life, gave believers a way to relate their faith to the demands of human reason. This eliminated any false separation of religious truth from human truth. A long line of writers and preachers brought the best of ancient culture to the service of Jesus Christ.

This process came to its climax in the great Catholic thinker, St. Thomas Aquinas, who helped his generation not to fear the newly discovered texts of Aristotle—which seemed to many a threat to the faith—but rather to show how the insights of truth really strengthen the Catholic faith. Following Thomas, every generation of Catholics has produced thinkers who have adopted a positive stance toward human truth. For Catholics, as a result of this tradition, truth is never something to fear.

The Galileo Affair: The Church and Science

When it comes to science, many people immediately think of the Catholic Church with reference to Galileo—

the way he has become the ultimate symbol of religion's inability to deal with scientific reality. Yet that image certainly is not the whole story, nor even the main theme. Pope John Paul II expressed regret for the misunderstandings surrounding the Galileo affair; even so, most people do not know the details of that incident, or the numbers of influential church leaders who subscribed to Galileo's novel ideas.

Two larger themes provide the context for the Galileo affair. One involves the broader story of how Aristotelian thinking was coming under pressure from new scientific observations about the physical world. Aristotle's own philosophy had arisen from numerous observations that he had made about a wide range of subjects, and his views had been accepted by religious thinkers and philosophers across all of Europe. Now things were changing—a whole world-view was shifting, and Galileo was only one piece of that.

The other thing to keep in mind is that religious people have been involved in the development of science since long before the time of Galileo, during his time, and long after it, even up until the present day. The accomplishments of Christian scientists were manifested in the construction of numerous cathedrals, which were as much triumphs of physics and engineering as well as tributes to God. Some of the greatest scientists were enormously committed followers of Jesus. Copernicus, the Polish scholar who first posited the theory that the earth revolves around the sun, was an Augustinian monk. Kepler, who formulated laws of the movement of planets around the sun, taught in a seminary and wanted to become a minister. Mendel, whose observations formed the basis of modern genetics, was also an Augustinian monk.

Whatever the historical conflicts of science and religion, the Catholic Church profoundly accepts the truths of science as science proposes them—as theories and concepts that will always demand greater precision, insight, and development. Our Church runs hundreds of universities where science and its attendant fields are taught and honored. It accepts the general outline of scientific concepts like evolution.

The Catholic Church, then, is hardly a society closed to culture or to science. In fact, it thrives on both.

This shows why our Church can uniquely contribute to the formation of your child. We affirm that believers function in the world as it is, with its realities, with its laws and principles, with its arts, and its creativity. By our commitment to education and truth, we have absorbed the great dimensions of human society over centuries, both in themselves and from the perspective of faith. This has formed an enormous, indisputable legacy of openness that we can pass on the future generations who will only flourish to the extent they have a similar openness.

Our Catholic openness to culture, art, and science arises from an even prior openness, one that has characterized our expression of Christian life from the beginning: a desire to reach out, engage, and become involved with "other kinds" of people.

The impulse to share faith cannot be fulfilled without a proportionate desire to meet people and become connected to them. For every story about faith through conquest, there are far more stories about faith through involvement and human exchange. St. Patrick's mission to Ireland arose from his abiding love for the Celtic people; violence did not characterize his mission—love did. When St. Augustine, the monk, was sent to England by Pope Gregory the Great (AD 595), it was the pope's fascination with the Anglo people whom he met in Rome that motivated him. What worked in Latin America was not so much the conquistadores and their love for New World gold, but the simple lives of the Franciscan, Dominican, and Jesuit missionaries who sought to evangelize the native people by enriching their lives—and, often, adapting to their cultural patterns.

Engaging with every culture involves, ultimately, a willingness to engage with every person. A desire to be present to others, to help them, to join with them, energizes every act of outreach. Power does not conquer; love, rather, breaks through.

This openness to humanity in all its breadth arises from the vision of the Kingdom—humankind united in love and service—bequeathed to the Church by Jesus.

It is nothing less than the extension of his love through time.

Vision and Mission

Faith makes a difference because our visions and hopes make a difference.

Consider how almost everything important that happened in your life came about because you had a vision, a sense of something that could be different, a hope.

Faith and hope break open our minds to other possibilities, other ways things can be, other ways of behaving and living.

Jesus, encouraging his followers to have ever deeper faith, gave his vision to the world through his followers. When, in the Scripture, a father brings his son possessed by a demon to Jesus (to us moderns it looks a lot like epilepsy) he says to Jesus, "But if you can do anything, have compassion on us and help us." Jesus replies with a passion we can still hear today: "'If you can!' Everything is possible for one who has faith" (Mark 9:22–24).

So what is faith?

Catholics have always taught faith is a gift, something that comes from God out of God's generosity. But that does not mean we cannot open ourselves up to receive faith more readily. Just as we can make faith more difficult by closing reality into airtight boxes that confine it, so we can make faith easier by realizing how open, fluid, and mystical everyday reality is.

We might think of faith this way: as a way to look at reality because of a trust we have come to have in God, in a transcendent Being and Reality beyond ourselves and our perceived experiences. Many things can lead us to open our hearts—the wonder of our child, for example; or the power of love; or the irrepressible drive of our minds; or our hopes for a fuller life for all human beings; or our need to find forgiveness and direction.

Having faith does not say we are stupid or infantile. Rather, it says that we have found our connection to all of creation, to all of existence, to all the possibilities of our existence, and to God who grounds and sustains existence, and who draws everything toward fullness.

Faith certainly involves trust because we realize that we ultimately cannot rely on ourselves and our powers, even though these point us toward the mystery of God. Faith also involves humility in that it calls us to estimate ourselves as we truly are, suspended between nothingness and eternity as the great French mathematician, Blaise Pascal, put it (1623–1662).

Indeed life can be curious and exciting without faith—there's no doubt about that. But without faith, we puzzle over questions we cannot resolve. We cannot figure out how human life emerged from random patterns of atoms; we cannot understand our ultimate drives—to love and know fully. We cannot really make sense out of death, unless we see it only as relief from unrelievable pain. Without faith, we can exalt in human reality, but we cannot probe its edges.

Faith gives perspective to all these unanswerable questions, not by providing fables and myths, but by giving us the gift of perspective, a way to see human life from beyond human life; a way to address irresolvable issues like sin, social dysfunction, and death; a way to bring into focus the amazing beings that we are.

With faith, we can see further. With faith we have a vision with an ever expanding horizon. With faith, we can make our way out of the maze.

This is not to say that faith answers everything or makes us know-it-alls. Rather, faith gives us a vision so deep and powerful that we stand humbled before it.

Jesus and the Holy Spirit

While faith has these transcendent qualities, it basically centers on the concrete—for a Christian, on Jesus Christ whose whole life revealed dimensions of God in such a way that God has become accessible to everyone. When Jesus calls God "Abba," (Mark 14:36) or "Daddy," and draws us into intimate trust and love of God; when Jesus expresses the care of God in powerful and personal ways; when Jesus gives himself in sacrifice and absolute trust to reveal the ultimate will of God—the restoration of humankind—this draws God with lines we can clearly see.

Even believers rarely reflect on how we assert that Jesus is the "exact imprint of God's very being" (Hebrews 1:3). So the boldness, the mercy, the compassion, the acceptance of the lowest in society and the scorned—these are not the peculiar acts of a religious fanatic, but rather the revelation of the inner being of God by Jesus. When Jesus loves, it is God loving; when Jesus heals, it is God healing. When Jesus dies, it is God sacrificing, that is, giving divine being on behalf of all of humanity.

Jesus' miracles and bold actions push the envelope of our experience. He insists on total trust when we pray because this is the only way we push beyond the assumptions we make about life, and life's limitations. He insists on radical reliance on God because this is the only way we can come to grips with the reality of God. He forces us into the ever-generous heart of God.

The total trust into which Jesus invites us has two effects which we see in his ministry: deeds of wonder and deeds of justice. These deeds are interconnected because both cause us to see the powerful presence of God who rights what is wrong, who heals what is broken, who loves what seems unlovable, who forgives those who feel unforgiven. When we come to trust totally, we become free to live at the deepest dimensions of existence.

Modern people are disposed to dismiss miracles as fantasies, as magical thinking that butts against the rigors of modern science. Jesus' public ministry did not consist of finding ways to violate the laws of nature. Rather, his career pointed to a depth and horizon in human experience where God becomes less hidden, more transparent. "Miracle" means "sign," "wondrous work," "something to be seen." The miracles of Jesus all call attention to a reality of God that people mostly cannot see.

Prayer brings us to depths of reality which, most of the time, we ignore or overlook. Left to ourselves, we run through our agendas, take care of daily needs and enjoy some diversion in life. Prayer invites us beneath and beyond this. Can it be that when we open ourselves up more deeply, we see and experience reality differently? Can it be that healing, peace, forgiveness, and justice are really all around us—but we need someone like Jesus to show us?

The less we think of miracles as magic and the more we think of them as wondrous signs, the more they line up with Jesus' teachings about how we relate to others. For our compassion, our openness to the poor, our desire to help the disenfranchised, our need to lift up those on the bottom—these too are wondrous signs of divine being and presence. These too, show God. Who can doubt that the defeat of decades-old segregation in the United States during the 1960s helped us see God more clearly? Who can doubt that the rejection of apartheid, long woven into South African culture, made the world see God—and life—more fully? Who can deny that the giving of food to the starving, hope to the despairing, and joy to the sorrowing, are all righting of what needs fixing, all manifestations of God's presence?

Jesus gives us a fresh, ever new, image of God, opening up for us, at the same time, new visions for ourselves. Personally and as a human community, God brings transformation.

Of course, this kind of activity on the part of Jesus did not always win him friends. In fact, for deep social, political, and religious reasons, many leaders at the time of Jesus were offended at what he said and did. His goodness evoked rage in return. Every one of us has experienced a tiny bit of this in our own lives: having done good, others took it the wrong way—or even resented it.

Paradoxically, this opposition leads to the greatest sign of God—the greatest miracle, if you will. Opposition to Jesus led to those events that Catholics call "the Paschal Mystery"—the death and resurrection of Jesus. Believers have to think of these two events as one—the one dramatic act where history and human meaning are torn open and the fullness of life is revealed.

The very attempt to silence and stop Jesus' revelation of God's life, of God's promised Kingdom, brings about its most powerful revelation. In the face of the greatest rage and rejection, in the face of one of the most brutal forms of human death, in the face of all the evil humans will do to each other—and even to God—because of sin's power in us, God conquers evil in the resurrection of his Son, Jesus.

In this act of dying and rising, we are well beyond philosophical consolations like "immortality of the soul," or stoic assurances that "we have our brief moments and then pass on." The death of Jesus forces us to face the plain, despicable fact of our own deaths. It cries to God for justice, redress, reversal. Death, rather than being just some natural outcome of aging body cells or some unwanted pathology, is the very insult to human existence itself.

To test this out, ask what you really want for your child? For the ones you love the most? Their very existence makes a claim on reality itself: their goodness, their uniqueness, the surprise of their being: these realities, we feel, cannot be snuffed out. Everything about us says this.

The Paschal Mystery of the death and resurrection of Jesus, then, functions as far more than some nice covering of reality, some pleasant denial of plain old unpleasant facts. Instead, it directly addresses the fact of human death in its graphically worse presentation—the crucifix—and from that depth of emptiness, reveals divine power over evil. Jesus, alone of all world religious figures, deals with the death that defines, in some way, every moment of our lives.

One often hears the formula, "Jesus died for us." But Christian faith pushes us beyond this. More than his death, Jesus' resurrection completes the essential step toward human redemption. Catholics, for sure, almost always show Jesus hung on the cross—sometimes other Christians dislike this—not because Jesus' death is the only thing that matters. Jesus' death happened for the sake of the resurrection, of the manifestation of a fullness of life whose hope haunts us even more than death. Every fiber of our being cries out for fuller life. Every moment of our existence pushes toward something more. Every death asserts an indomitable desire for greater life.

It is the resurrection of Jesus that frames Christian life—how it makes Christ now available, in his transcendent state, to all of human history, how it shapes the outline of Christian life because we live "in the risen Lord," and, most importantly, how it leads to the bestowal of the Holy Spirit upon us.

Although many Christians usually think of Jesus as the Son of God, they often overlook the Spirit of God. The Holy Spirit is that dimension of divine being that unites with us so as to bring power, transformation, consolation and love. It is through the Spirit that the work of Jesus—revealing and bringing the Kingdom of God—continues throughout history. Our lives as Catholics receive as much from the Spirit as they do from the Son of God.

We probably all have some memory of the story of Pentecost in the book of Acts (chapter 2) when the disciples felt wind sweep through the upper room, saw tongues of flame come over their heads, and knew something dramatic had happened. They go out from their house to the crowds and begin speaking; although they are speaking Aramaic with a Galilean accent, people from all different cultures hear them.

What St. Luke has done is represent in this scene the early Christians' experience of the Holy Spirit—bringing them beyond their fear, bringing them into contact with many cultures, and enabling people to proclaim their faith and form communities of faith. St. Luke has, like all the New Testament writers, a very dynamic conception of the Holy Spirit. Paul fills out the experience of the Spirit when he talks about gifts that people receive to build up the community of Christ, and virtues that the Spirit brings about in believers. These virtues are abiding powers that reside in such a way in believers and are ready at hand for believers to exercise as needed.

Catholics count faith, hope, and love as the greatest virtues of the Spirit, but also many other virtues like faithfulness, peace, joy, wisdom, and prudence, generosity and profound respect for God (that is, making God first of all in one's life). Everyone might look into his or her heart and see if the Spirit has begun to implant these virtues by which Christians live in faithfulness to Christ.

Ultimately, the role of the Spirit is to conform believers to Jesus more and more clearly, until they have the mind of Christ, seeing as Christ sees.

Jesus and the Spirit bestow upon believers the vision and mission to live for the Kingdom of God, for the sway of divine love and life in all of human experience. That vision, to be sure, is not basically sectarian. The vision of

Jesus expands to all humankind, relating all people to God's love and life.

A Way of Life

Although it might not seem obvious to people who have not grown up Catholic, Catholicism, more than anything else, is a way of life. It is not just a creed, or a large institution, or an organization on the global or local levels, or some historical relic. Catholicism becomes a perspective through which people see things, and a set of values out of which people act.

A sense of union with God lies at the heart of the Catholic experience—reinforced not only through the Eucharist (Mass) but in daily life, in the connection Catholics feel between themselves, their world, and God. God, known in the experience of his love and power, forms the foundation of the lives of Catholics, as familiar to them as they are to themselves. Catholics may not overtly pray like some orthodox Jewish people. They may not bow down to the East as Muslims do, making homage five times a day. But Catholics have their lives permeated with a sense of the divine, of God being part of their everyday experience, of being intimately in dialogue with God.

Catholics have a variety of ways of formally praying. Many say set morning and evening prayers; many pause at lunchtime for quiet prayer. Millions say the Rosary because Mary encapsulates so much of the simple life, attuned to God, that Catholics instinctually feel. Millions stop in churches for quiet moments of prayer before the

Eucharist, the consecrated bread, which we believe is the Body of Christ, reserved in church for use during the week, particularly to bring Communion to the sick. Millions read the Bible and meditate on a few verses at various times during the day. Growing numbers gather into small groups to share their sense of God and God's direction in the lives.

Family life, too, becomes an opportunity for creating an ambiance of prayer for our children and families. Simple prayers in the morning, prayers over meals, a scripture story shared in the evening culminating in night-time prayer, can make for a rhythmic world ordered toward God.

Catholics, for sure, need to be more explicit in their prayer because they keep their witness to God largely private and personal (except when they are at church). But Catholics feel God around them and within them—a fountain of love and strength.

Out of this sense of God come the moral actions of Catholic people. Catholics have, like most groups, notorious sinners who bring shame upon us. We all fall short. But the average Catholic tries to live with honesty, integrity, respect for life and people, and a sense of caution when temptation lurks. An instinctual generosity and compassion arises in Catholic hearts, particularly toward neighbors and those who have less. Catholic moral teaching does not change as fads do; rather, a core of values which have run through Christian experience from the beginning guides the teaching of Catholic leaders and the behavior of everyday Catholics.

Many Catholics think about their moral lives in terms of the Ten Commandments. The first three commandments order our lives to God, affirming God as the absolute center of our lives and loyalty. Our weekly lives, which includes the Lord's Day as a day of rest and reflection, embody this relationship—hence the importance of Sunday worship. The last seven commandments cover our relationships with others—caring for family, upholding truth, being faithful to our vows and living with sexual integrity.

The Ten Commandments, though, cannot capture the *positive* dimension of Catholic moral life—the way we are called to care for others as God cares for us, as Jesus shows us the love of God. Here moral life does not revolve around what minimum is required; rather, it asks: how can I show God's abundant love in a particular situation. We can just imagine what a perspective like this can bring to daily life, in our families, neighborhoods, schools, businesses, and broader public life.

One can read books such as the *Catechism of the Catholic Church* or the *United States Catholic Catechism for Adults,* which formalize all of Catholic teaching, prayer, and spirituality. Far better, though, to see it alive in Catholic people, in the sheer decency of the lives of everyday believers.

Discipleship

We return here to a theme we saw in Part I—how *discipleship*, the following of Jesus in a personal, committed way, can bring a solid basis to how we understand ourselves and relate to others.

When the Church offers us a vision of discipleship, it is a way to sum up all that it can bring to believers' lives today. Discipleship calls us beyond a generic identity with our nationality and family heritage to a fuller acceptance of Jesus Christ in our lives. As a result, it provides a way to grasp and express what faith has to offer people today.

Discipleship has four bases: the Word of God, the prayerful expression of our relationship with God, community, and service. Each of these bases reinforces the others, giving Catholics today a vision of what it means to believe.

The Word of God

The twentieth century completed a revolution in Catholic life, the culmination of centuries of deeper study of the Bible. Of course the Bible has been at the center of Catholic treasures since the time of Jesus; the New Testament sprang from the experience and witness of the first followers of Jesus over the course of many decades. Catholic liturgy has enshrined the Scripture, and made it accessible to people, throughout all of our history. Our cathedrals have portrayed the Scripture in vividly-tinted stained glass for centuries.

But the twentieth-century pulled together advances in translation, technology, historical studies, and ancient texts to allow Catholics a greater understanding of the Scriptures, and also greater access to them in modern language. Catholic scholars have contributed on an equal level with Protestant and Jewish scholars to open the ancient world up to modern believers.

In addition, the Church revised the texts that are read at Mass, giving Catholics just about every substantial passage of the Scriptures at Sunday Mass over a three-year cycle. This means that the Scriptures now constitute the basic input for Catholic imagination and spirituality. We walk around with the Scripture ringing in our heads!

As a result, the Word of God clarifies our relationship with God more clearly. As we hear of God's action and love, we are called to respond. The Scripture insists that we not be passive, but open, and change our hearts in accord with God's message.

In other words, the Scripture calls us to conversion.

As we are brought into clearer relationship with God—Father, Son, and Spirit—through Jesus Christ, so we must answer the question: what does Jesus mean in our lives? Will we accept him? Will we follow him? What church community will support us most in our ongoing conversion?

After all, conversion is not done once and forever. Conversion is ongoing.

Expression

If we have a relationship, we must express it in some way.

Relationships cannot be private, hidden, suppressed. Rather, we must show them in order for them to retain any semblance of reality. How can we have a relationship with someone and never express the connection we have?

Employees report to employers. Organizations take care of their clients. Businesses provide for their customers. Friends keep in contact with friends. Parents relate to their children in different ways as their children grow. Lovers express their love to each other.

So how do we express the relationship we have with God? With the personal God of love that Jesus reveals? With the Trinity of life and generosity at the core of Christian belief? Catholics name the fullness of God that Jesus revealed "The Holy Trinity," which recognizes the richness, depth, and relationship that Jesus revealed through his life. Saying "Father," "Son," and "Spirit" does not mean that there are three gods. Rather one God is expressed in the richness of Father, Son, and Spirit.

We express our relationship with God through prayer—personal prayer and prayer as a community of believers. As we have deep communion with a friend, sharing ourselves through the sharing of words and ideas, so the communion we have with God the Father, Jesus the Son, and the Holy Spirit, becomes real in the experience of praying.

Personal prayer, at least in the form of a dialogue with God, comes naturally to most Catholics. We associate important dimensions of our lives with God, and we visit those dimensions (our hopes, values, loves, fears, etc.) as we go through life. Often personal prayer arises from anguish and pain. To whom can we cry out in our need? This drives us to deeper reliance on God. Often, too, our personal prayer shows itself in adoration and praise. We have come to encounter the mystery of unlimited love, of unbounded generosity, as the source of our lives. We see beauty, truth, goodness, and grace. As we meet God this way, we feel only an awe that leads us to cry "Alleluia!"

As we grow as disciples, our prayer has to get more regular. We need distinct times of the day that we set aside for prayer. These set times bring order to our relationship with God. When families, and sometimes friends, engage in these set times, it becomes a form of group formation, of disciples supporting disciples on our journey.

The Mass, along with the other sacraments, is our fullest form of group prayer, of disciples supporting other disciples in faith. Catholics, with Eastern Orthodox and some Protestant believers, count seven sacraments (Baptism, Confirmation, Eucharist, Reconciliation, Anointing of the Sick, Holy Orders, and Marriage), but the fundamental ones are Baptism and Eucharist. Baptism, the beginning of discipleship, serves as the doorway to all other prayer and worship.

Catholics hold that weekly Mass, on Sunday as the day of the Lord's resurrection, forms a necessary and indispensable part of Catholic discipleship. The Mass means far more than receiving Communion. At Mass we hear God's Word again, are called to conversion and commitment, affirm our dependence on God and our personal love of Christ, become one with the Lord's self-offering in love, unite with Jesus in the Eucharist, and receive the commission to live our faith throughout the week.

You will often hear about this Catholic practice of worshipping on Sunday (or Saturday evening) because

(a) there is no other resource Catholics can substitute for the essential values of the Mass—not any personal prayer, not any walks in the woods or meditations; and (b) modern attitudes often make attendance at Mass difficult. Many believers suffer in profound ways because they do not participate in the Eucharist and skip Sunday Mass. As a result, they walk around deprived and malnourished—most of the time not even realizing it!

For Catholics, attendance at Mass should be the highest priority; we strongly commend attendance at Mass for Catholics as a family. If you are not a Christian or Catholic, we realize that Sunday Mass may not make sense. However, even though you do not regularly attend Sunday Mass, it will help you to realize the importance of the Mass for your child's friends and associates in school, because of how it permeates our Catholic lives.

Community

Modern ideas about nations presumed that we were all isolated individuals who then come together to form a society.

In this regard, Catholic attitudes are dramatically un-modern!

Catholics believe we are created as communal beings, inherently connected to each other. We all have a part to play in community because, without community, human reality is not possible. Everything about us, from our inner world to our external actions, happens in the context of community.

Through the community of family we receive our most personal and abiding identities. Society then shapes and expands these identities through the interplay we have with other children, school, adolescent and young adult peers, friendships and infatuations, loves and commitments—all taking place in the vortex of broader social patterns that sweep through cultures.

Mutual obligations exist as a result of the social creatures we are. Society owes us, at least for the fundamental needs of human life. But we likewise owe society, to support and enhance it, to contribute our gifts and talents, and to work with others to create a common good that supports everyone. Some of this, for sure, smacks against certain strains of individuality that arise in American life from now and then. But once the interplay between societies and its members becomes broken, we enter a world that is indeed savage and selfish.

Your child, in coming to us, comes to a community. By extension and by osmosis, we, in partnership with you, will imbue the values of community in your child. To the extent your child grows in knowing profound connectedness with others, to that extent we will have been successful.

The community of the Catholic Church is broad and diverse. People relate to us in different ways. Some connect with us tangentially, through some services we offer for a specific need. Others are involved more consistently because their children are part of our education system. Some feel a sense of belonging to us, expressing this through a desire to baptize a child. Others feel very much a part of our community, becoming involved in parish life on a regular basis, as worshippers and, even more, as volunteers and ministers.

It seems undeniable, however, that most people today expect powerful community connections with their churches. This comes, in part, from the great isolation people feel in today's world, and also from the stronger language of community and discipleship that today's believers use.

Just as community affects who we are as persons, it also affects who we are as believers. Belief, in its beginning or its ongoing growth, does not fall magically from heaven. Belief comes from God, but it invariably comes through other believers, from communities, from churches and, indeed, from the Catholic Church. God uses community to open us to grace. How we let the community of the Church, as neighbors, friends, and believers, into our lives can indeed transform our own faith, and that of our children.

Service

The Gospel has a purpose, the same purpose as Jesus—the bringing of the Kingdom of God more powerfully into human experience. For more than a century, religious thinkers have described Jesus as "a man for others"—trying to capture the way he lives in service, particularly for the outcast, the underclass, the isolated, the unforgiven.

Sometimes our own experience of God can appear to be for ourselves. We feel so relieved, so cleansed, so joyful, so enthralled, or ecstatic, that we want to preserve that moment. This typical religious sentiment affected the apostles too. Taken onto a mountain to experience the glory of Jesus, Peter cries out to no one in particular, "Lord it is good to be here. Let us build three tents." Peter and his companion apostles, James and John, wanted to bask in the glory of Jesus. Immediately, however, the apostles see a cloud descend on them, and a voice speaking, "This is my beloved Son, listen to him" (Mark 9:7). Then they descend down the mountain; during the descent, Jesus mentions his impending death and resurrection.

You can't stay on the mountain, no matter how "high" the experience. God loves the poor, to those most in need—this is the consistent message of the Scriptures, from God's appearance to Moses, through all the prophets, right into the ministry of Jesus.

Catholics engage in service on a variety of levels. As a large organization, few can match the array of hospitals, clinics, charitable outlets, and schools, all of them non-profit, all of them run at significant financial sacrifice. As you learn more about the Catholic community, you will find layers of service that make up the fabric of Catholic charities.

On a personal level, too, Catholics have multiple opportunities through—and beyond—their parish to roll up their sleeves, spend a chunk of time, and express the love of God to others in some particular way. While many give hours for religious education or visitation of the sick at home, many also give their time to serving in food kitchens for the poor or homeless shelters, to tutoring or raising funds. An ideal Catholic Church (and we are not there yet!) would have every Catholic giving his or her time to serve in some way beyond their own family circle.

We have reviewed, even if briefly, a sweeping vision of what the Catholic Church offers people today—a community, committed to furthering every human person, in a spirit of openness and love, through the vision and mission that Jesus gave us and the Spirit reinforces. This leads to a way of life which we call discipleship, rooted in God's Word, in prayer and worship, in community, and in service.

In some way, your child will be touched by all of these dimensions of the Catholic vision, surely at different times and with different force. Your child will absorb parts of this vision in unique ways, depending on his or her disposition and background. How rich this vision becomes for your child depends on many factors, some of which cannot be known. But one clear factor is the child's own family and its openness to this vision of faith.

As part of our introduction of the Catholic community to you, we've asked you, in part 1, "What do you really want?" because often we are seeking even more than we consciously suspect. And then we've sketched, in part 2, a bit of what we, as a Catholic people, have to offer you.

We think this moment in your life is special because your child and family life is presenting opportunities which sometimes we do not notice. All of life opens up with the coming and growing of a young child—all the ways life can be, or be better…and how faith can make life better.

Thank you, once again, for your trust in us. When it comes to what we can do for you, please do not be bashful in your asking.

Now it's time to talk a little bit about the way we partner with each other for the good of your child.

Points to Ponder

1. What, if anything, surprised you in this chapter?

2. What are some of the elements in the Catholic culture that were not a part of your culture growing up?

3. Do you have any questions about what you read in this chapter? If so, what?

4. How would you answer the question, "What does it mean to be Catholic?"

Three

Feeling at Home with the Catholic Community

W e are inviting you to partner with us, the Catholic community.

We know that people come to us at various different points in their lives. Wherever you are, we want you to feel at home with the Catholic family.

Feeling on Board

A strong percentage of parents today are fully on board with the Catholic family of faith. Born and raised Catholic, they have weathered the late teen and young adult years and come out stronger in their Catholic faith and identity. Bringing a child to the Church means passing on a strong faith to their child.

Sometimes society looks at this as "not giving your child a choice." Catholics look upon raising one's child in the faith as giving one's child the basic nourishment that the child needs. Should faith be viewed as some kind of extra, even unnecessary, part of life that one can dispense

48

with? Or should faith be seen as something like language, food, and basic care? Catholics think that faith is more important than anything else because it orients a child to what is fundamental in life and gives a child a relationship that will sustain a whole host of other relationships.

If you can identify with the Catholic faith in this basic, on-board way, we invite you to complete a partnership as soon as possible for your child. This does not mean that *you work with us* in the formation of your child. Indeed, you, the parents, have the primary role in the raising, formation, education, and evangelization of your child. So *our* role is to *work with you!*

Probably the hardest challenge to being a parent today revolves around balancing the competing demands in life and finding perspective and proportion. Between work, school, transportation, friends, and family demands, it can look like there is little time for anything. When the pressures start, strangely, the more important things—our closest relationships and our relationship with God—start getting the short end of the deal.

Think about the people you admire most. Invariably, they get your attention because they keep family and faith at the top of their priorities. Other responsibilities find their place within these primary ones.

With a solid commitment to living your faith, you can use the Catholic community as a strong resource in your life. Our patterns of prayer, regular Scripture selections, Sunday Mass, opportunities to connect with and serve others, and our moral vision can all become part of the way you address life with your family. You can move from thinking of yourself as a volunteer to thinking of yourself as a participant in the life of Jesus, living this out through faith. You can move more closely to thinking of yourself as a disciple.

The Church, to be sure, has no interest in religious fanaticism, or in making all its members into church mice. Discipleship, for Catholics, does not look like that. Rather, the strength that we receive from our active faith life, nourished by various levels of prayer, calls us out beyond the walls of the Church into the various worlds of family, friends, neighborhood, workplace, and community. Just as Jesus engaged people in homes and in streets, Jesus calls us to be disciples of the Gospel in our everyday world.

We make our invitation to deepen your sense of being Catholic primarily for what it will do for you, your child, and your family. We believe that your life will be enriched and supported so powerfully that you will forever be grateful for the fuller life that God has given you and your family.

Feeling Almost on Board

Sociologists of religion tell us of a growing phenomenon today, people who have some residual identity with a faith but do not totally connect with it. One term for this kind of person is *liminals*, people who, in the imagery of that word, stand at the doorway but don't entirely enter.

We know there are many factors behind this trend— notably, the sheer way people grow up today with multiple options and a seemingly endless stretch of time to "find themselves." Beginning in high school, college becomes almost an experimental canvas for many people, with the post-college years serving as extensions of the search for oneself.

During this period, people experiment with many different environments, sets of friends, and career possibilities, not to mention potential partners and lovers. As a result, commitment to many things in life seems provisional, and commitments to anything set (like one's career-track or even one's religion) become tentative.

But this extended state of exploration cannot go on forever. Life starts making demands, and commitments start becoming necessary because we cannot keep love, family, and settling down at bay forever. We meet someone who changes our lives and begins to claim our total attention. We commit ourselves and begin thinking about family. We settle into careers because we need the steady income—and because we've often found the set of issues that really engages our skills. And we start setting up the nest that will define our lives for many years.

Sociologists tell us that involvement in church often accompanies this process of settling down. And it's easy to see why.

When we have children, we really start to deal with the ultimate values that are important to us because these values and ideals will shape what we pass on to our children. How we live, what's important to us, how we show and share love, how we treat others, how we approach work, and how we look forward to the future—these texture our lives. They serve as living "wallpaper" for us. Most importantly, they become the background for the assumptions our children will carry through life.

So bringing a child for Baptism, religious education, or full Catholic School education, does not come out of the blue. It springs from a matrix of values that are now being acted upon—now being actualized when we become parents.

Our invitation is for you to reflect upon how Catholic values can help clarify and strengthen the values that you already have—and how strengthening of those values will greatly enhance what you are trying to accomplish for your child.

The more your child sees you as part of their school-education-faith-formation experience, the more that experience will impact on their lives. Children need to see coherence between school, family, friends, church, and values; if they do not, they have to work harder to make sense of everything.

Everyone comes at things at a different pace, but we hardly stand still in life. Your reflection on family and faith may take quite a while, but it can hardly stand still. As you solidify your values and commitments at this point in your life, the Catholic community of faith will continue to be available as a resource for you and your child.

Jesus always extends the invitation to deeper faith and discipleship.

Feeling Nearby

Some people come to the Catholic community with values very much aligned with those of the Catholic people, even though they may not be Catholic themselves.

Catholic educators have long noted that people of other Christian, or even non-Christian, expressions of faith have nevertheless wanted their child to be exposed to Catholic values. This happens in a parish-based religious education when a parent or grandparent is Catholic, but a parent or parents are not. It mostly involves wanting a child to be in a Catholic school, or perhaps being involved in a Vacation Bible School for children during the summer.

You undoubtedly admire many things in the Catholic Church—our educational system, our valuing of each child, our religious environment, our emphasis on discipline and focus, our broad community of good-minded people. There may even be some personal connection to the Catholic community—a relative who is Catholic, or neighbors, or living near a parish.

We invite you to engage with us as much as is comfortable and possible. It's a privilege for us to serve you and have a place in the life of your child.

There will be times when your child may be involved in various activities that take place in the church building. It may be around Thanksgiving, Christmas or some other holiday; or it may be around a commencement celebration. We will be very sensitive to your child's participation with the other children during these moments.

While your child may not be able to be part of all the activity of the children (if, for example, the children are preparing for Holy Communion or some other formal church ritual), we will do everything in our power to help your child feel included in an appropriate way and part of the service. It is only natural for children to want to do what other children are doing, particularly if they see the activity as a point of pride. They do not want to be left out.

There are, however, many ways in which children can participate and be made to feel part of the ceremony even if they are not exactly doing what the Catholic children are doing. They can read the Scripture, or help with some of the altar activities, or be part of the singing. However this might work out in detail, we hope you will encourage your child to take part in these events, and that you will feel connected to them yourself.

In this situation, please feel free to speak up! Let us know what your concerns are, how your child is feeling or thinking about things, and what ways we can make your child feel most included in the service. Even though some people may not be able to receive Holy Communion (which for us Catholics is the ultimate sign of unity in faith), everyone can use this sacred moment to experience spiritual communion with Jesus. The Sacrament makes his love known, but the Sacrament does not restrict his love.

Many parishes today will encourage people who are not ready to receive Holy Communion to come forward in the Communion line and ask for a blessing from the minister, with their arms across their chests in the form of an "x." Children not old enough to receive Communion as well as Protestant friends visiting the Catholic parish often come forward for such a blessing.

Whenever you can, please feel free to come to church or school and be part of the religious activities, to the extent that you feel comfortable. Your presence helps to reinforce the values that your child experiences every day, and will help your child integrate these values into his or her life.

Feeling a Little Further Away

Some people choose to send their children to the Catholic community for specific benefits, even though they feel they have little explicit connection with the Catholic Church. Many belong to another Christian tradition, or to non-Christians expressions of faith. Some may even feel they don't believe in any divine reality. Even so, many still see the particular opportunities that the Catholic environment provides their children, irrespective of faith. Sometimes it is the educational values; sometimes the social values dominate, particularly if it is in the area of art or sports.

Even though parents in this situation might feel little explicit kinship with the Catholic family, we will do everything we can to make you, and particularly your child, feel at home. While there may be little desire to adopt Catholic practices or beliefs, every parent should know that their child will be accepted and loved as every other child is.

Jesus taught us that all children see a dimension of his Kingdom because of the simplicity and purity of their vision.

Your child may feel awkward at times because she or he is not Catholic or Christian. Your child will be in an environment in which prayer, the Scripture, and talk of God will be part of her or his life. This will inevitably create in your child some sense of kinship with the other children, and a desire to be like them, and do religious practices like them.

We believe we can create an environment that is authentically Catholic and Christian, but still provide the space your child needs to be different without feeling separated. As we articulate Catholic beliefs and values, we will build bridges between them and the values that your family upholds. We believe Jesus' message has universal values which can enrich the world of everyone. While holding on to our beliefs, we will reinforce virtues important to you.

When it comes to explicit Catholic practices like receiving Holy Communion, we know this may place extra tension on your child, even more so than on other Christian children who are not Catholic. We will dialogue with you to see ways in which your child, and your family, can be part of these events which are so important for Catholic children and families. Openness, with a profound affirmation of the good will everyone has, will show us a way.

At the same time, we encourage you to reflect on our Catholic and Christian values, those we expressed in part 2 of this book, if only to find some reflection of your own religious or human values. After all, these qualities in our Catholic life have drawn you to decide to become involved with us. You have come to us not as strangers, but as friends and partners.

Points to Ponder

1. What if any are the ways you wish the Church could better accommodate you or your child?

2. Identify what you believe are your own values and identify what you believe are Catholic values. What do you notice about these two lists?

3. What value do you now see in your child being affiliated with the Church?

Four

You, Us, and God

G od is not done with me yet.
This well-used adage touches on a profound truth, the incomplete state of our lives at virtually any point. If life is something like a journey, then we are always heading somewhere—heading to another point which we've not yet reached.

A view of life like this can seem like endless restlessness—as if we cannot sit still, appreciate the life we have, and "stop to smell the roses," as folks always advise us to do. A view like this can play into a certain immaturity, a certain acceptance of responsibilities within the limitations which are always part of any life.

But seeing life as a journey can also speak of life's openness, its capacity to change and grow, its need to advance further.

How strange that we can look back in life and see it as an almost inevitable working out of past decisions and options. Yet, at the same time, at any point we can be looking ahead and see only endless possibilities.

God is not done with us yet, because there are always new possibilities in our lives. These arise from our complex connections with others and the multiple opportunities that surround us, once we open our eyes. Every time someone has the feeling that she or he is "stuck" somewhere, inevitably that person just has not looked around, opened their eyes, and seen the alternatives.

This does not mean there are not commitments, responsibilities, or chosen paths. Rather, within our commitments, possibilities, and chosen paths still lay numerous possibilities that often are only limited by our imagination.

So we don't have to be exactly the way we are. We can attend more fully to other people. We can reflect more on our lives. We can let ourselves be affected more. Or escape from our destructive patterns. Or reach out to people we've long dismissed. Or pray a little more regularly. Or be more present during tough times with those we love.

Life may not be totally fluid, but it certainly is not carved in stone.

This may be nowhere more relevant than in our relationship with God. We have images of God that go back to our earliest years—words and feelings associated with circumstances surrounding our childhood. Perhaps our mothers taught us to pray. Perhaps we went to pre-K religious education. Perhaps we were at Sunday school or made First Holy Communion. How much the sentiments of those years still continue to shape our lives!

Often people grow, mature, and nuance every part of their lives—except their lives of faith. They stay with images of God from their childhood such as an old man in the sky, or some diffuse cloud, or some heavenly force. Indeed, even these images might be useful at times in our lives—when we are in crisis we cling to anything—but they may not be so helpful for sustaining a mature relationship with God as the intelligent, self-aware persons we have become.

Of course we will revert to simpler images when we talk to children. God cannot be known apart from images, and the simpler ones work for children, given their level of understanding. But they may no longer work for us—to think of some matterless brain floating in the sky, or some old man inclined to be grumpy, or some unconnected bit of energy, simply leaves us empty.

The greatest mystics in the Catholic tradition learned this. Saints John of the Cross and Teresa of Avila, both Spaniards who lived in the sixteenth century, understood that God gradually purifies our minds until we arrive at images of God that come closer to reality—granted we can never grasp that reality completely.

How do we conceive of endless, infinite love? Of abundant gift? Of living totally for others? Of perfect wisdom? Of a personal Being who holds all other being in existence? Of a personal Being who transcends our notions of what it means to be a person? The greatest mystics got as close as they could to the mystery and tried to abide in its fullness.

How do we conceive of a God who reveals divine Being in Jesus, one born in our midst, whose perfections include compassion, mercy, kindness, and peace? Jesus has to use parables to move us closer to his vision of God.

What can we do except refine our own parables of God?

These parables, these initial images, will come from our intuitions of God's presence from our earliest years, from the sense we've had of something and Someone beyond ourselves, from the feelings we have of being guided in our lives. We've all gone through situations that we know should have taken our lives. We've stared out across endless seas and into brilliant sunsets. We've all embraced those we love, trembling at the sheer beauty and frailty of our existence, knowing that these kinds of moment touch on the eternal.

These kinds of images can guide us to a faith that moves us forward in our understanding of God and our acceptance of God's love in our lives. These kinds of parables—from our own lives—amplified by the Word of God can help us discern deeper patterns for ourselves and those we love. These kinds of intimations of God can throw light on the journey we are privileged to walk.

So where might God be leading you?

What might be the next steps in your journey?

What invitation to faith sits unopened on your desk or tabletop?

We Are Here

Your Catholic community is here most of all to serve you.

Our concern, of course, is for your child.

But our concern includes you as well, because we partner with you in serving the growth of your child. So we are here to be of service to you.

We certainly encourage you to become involved with other parents. Sometimes parent groups might be fairly organized; sometimes informal groups start to develop on their own. Nothing can beat peer support and sharing. The sharing will range over a wide field, including our children, family issues, and how faith intersects with these.

If you'd ever like time to chat with personnel from the school or the parish community, just call us up at the school, religious education office, or the church rectory. We will keep your conversation confidential; we will do whatever we can to address your concerns.

If you'd like to know more about the Catholic faith, we have resources for you. We have shorter and longer books for your reflection. We'd be happy to talk to you in one-on-one conversation. And we have a program of introduction to the Catholic Faith which we call "Inquiry." Even if someone does not decide to investigate the Catholic faith further, these sessions will be helpful just in terms of the information they provide.

If you are a Catholic but have been less active than you'd like, we would very much like to help you become more active. Sometimes this involves your natural desire to become involved in the faith formation of your child. Sometimes it might involve some sessions that help you review and revisit your faith. Sometimes it might involve talking out some feelings that go way back in life. Often, it will involve celebrating the Sacrament of Reconciliation or Penance (which is often called Confession) once again. We can make all of this easier for you.

If you are an active Catholic, we will help you grow in that faith, for the sake of your family and yourself. From ways of sharing the Scriptures, to various opportunities for service, to resources for family life, to involvement in the school, religious education program or parish—we can help facilitate many avenues to enhance your family's life. Of course, we have no greater resource than the Sunday Eucharist; nothing can enrich your family's life over the years as the sacred Food Jesus gives us in Word and Eucharist. But opportunities for daily prayer and family faith sharing can bring the power of the Mass into the daily life of your family.

Points to Ponder

So here you are, surrounded by opportunity and options:

1. Where do you want to go?
2. Where will God lead you?

Catholic Fun Facts

Cappuccino: Cappuccino is a great drink named after an order of friars! These friars were Franciscans, and, as the story goes, in the sixteenth century, there were friars who wore *capuches* (derived from *capuccio* meaning hood). Children would follow the new friars chanting "Cappucino, Cappucino." The now famous drink of espresso and steamed milk looked like the color of a "Capuchin's" clothing—like a "cappuccino."

Which Cardinal Came First? Most people assume that church leaders are called "Cardinals" because they wear the color of the bird. Not so. The princes of the Church were named first. Cardinals come from the word for "hinge," and a lot hinges on Cardinals. The College of Cardinals elects the pope!

How Many? Can you believe that there are over one billion Catholics that share this planet?

Coquilles Saint Jacques: Did you ever order Coquilles Saint Jacques? It is interesting to note that this great scallop dish is named for Saint James; in fact, you will find a scallop shell on the emblem of Saint James. Pilgrims who would journey to the shrine of Saint James often wore a scallop shell. The pilgrim would stop at a church, or a home, or an abbey and ask for a portion of food the size of the shell.

That would provide some sustenance for the pilgrim without the pilgrim becoming a burden to households of those with little or no means.

Five

Things Catholic
A Short Tour of Basic Catholic Stuff

S ometimes people want contact with the Catholic Church, but they feel uncomfortable because they are not familiar with many things that Catholics take for granted. Often this fear is unwarranted because, unfortunately, many younger Catholics are also unfamiliar with some traditional Catholic practices. Here's a short tour of some basic Catholic practices and arrangements to help you get oriented.

Catholic Organization

The whole Catholic world is organized into territorial areas called **dioceses**. An important area, from which other dioceses have been formed, is called an **archdiocese**. Each diocese, in turn, is composed of smaller territories called **parishes**; most Catholic parishes have specific territorial boundaries, even though these are not strictly adhered to in all circumstances.

Each diocese has a chief priest called a **bishop**; the bishop of an archdiocese is called an **archbishop**. The local priest in a parish is called the **pastor**. Another group of ministers, called **deacons**, serve both bishops and priests at Catholic services, but they also serve the needs of the poor in an explicit way.

The pope is the bishop of Rome, the diocese that Catholics consider the "mother diocese" and the most important church because St. Peter and St. Paul were each martyred there. Cardinals, chosen by the pope, assist him either in Rome or throughout the world. A pope serves until death or resignation—though only one pope has resigned in Christian history. Cardinals elect the next pope by secret ballot.

The local parish, which most Catholic relate to most often, may have another priest or two in service (called **parochial vicars**), and other **lay ecclesial ministers** in addition to any deacons. Lay ecclesial ministers are Catholics who receive special training to serve the Church, perhaps as religious educators or experts in another church field. Every parish also has several dozens of lay people who also serve in a variety of ways in the ministry of the parish.

Catholic Church Building

A local congregation constructs the local church building and any other parish buildings. It raises funds and provides the resources to erect the building. The pastor, in conjunction with his bishop and people in his parish, will make sure the building is properly constructed. (If he doesn't, his name will be unceremoniously invoked for decades to come!)

Catholic church buildings may be quite old and traditional, or they may be quite modern. Older buildings tend to be fairly ornate, while newer buildings tend to have cleaner lines. Nevertheless, every church has the same basic setup.

1) The Church focuses attention to the sanctuary where Catholics celebrate Mass. In this area the sanctuary includes the main altar, also a pulpit (called at times an *ambo*), and a chair for the priest presider at Mass. Catholics use the pulpit only to proclaim the Word of God, so its place in the sanctuary shows the importance of the Scripture for Catholics.

2) Every church also has a place for baptism. If that is an established, formal location, we call this a baptistery. Otherwise some churches have mobile fonts that they use for baptism.

3) Almost all churches have benches or pews. These have kneelers that Catholics use for the parts of the Mass when they kneel, although very rarely Catholic places of worship do not have kneelers and people may stand in place of kneeling.

4) Every Catholic church has a tabernacle, a more or less ornate box with a lock, in which it preserves the Holy Eucharist that was not consumed at Mass. (Catholics believe this bread remains the Body of Christ after it is consecrated—solemnly blessed.) The tabernacle may be in the main body of the church or in a reserved, special room. When Catholics enter a place where there is a tabernacle, they traditionally

genuflect, that is, they bend their right knee until it touches the ground, after which they rise.

5) Catholic churches also have vessels that contain holy water (water blessed as a reminder of baptism). These vessels may be as simple as small dishes, or they may be rather elaborate fountains with water pumped through them. Sometimes the fountain used for baptism is also used as a holy water vessel for people.

6) Catholics, when they enter church, touch the vessel with holy water and, with their finger wet, make the Sign of the Cross. People know Catholics perhaps most of all for this gesture in which Catholics touch their forehead, their abdomen, and their left and right shoulders while they say, "In the Name of the Father, and of the Son, and of the Holy Spirit. Amen." This one gesture reminds Catholics of (a) their redemption through the cross of Jesus; and (b) the God who saves us is Father, Son and the Holy Spirit—but still one God.

You should know, too, that we do not encourage athletes to make the sign of the cross to improve their sports abilities! However, some athletes do make the Sign of the Cross at certain times in their games as a reminder that, when all is said and done, whoever wins and loses, faith comes first.

Catholic Sacraments

Almost all Christians recognize two sacraments, baptism and Eucharist (the Mass). Along with the Catholic Church, the Orthodox Church and some

Protestant communities accept seven sacraments. A sacrament is a formal ritual action or sign through which believers experience in a particular way the saving power of God. Catholics think of sacraments as powerful gestures of Jesus Christ, done again through the Holy Spirit's presence in the Church. As Jesus touched and saved people in his life, so Catholics believe Jesus continues that through the sacraments.

Three sacraments begin and complete a believer's initiation into the Church.

> *Baptism*, which is the pouring of water over a person, and saying the formula, "I baptize you in the name of the Father, and of the Son, and of the Holy Spirit. Amen."

> *Confirmation*, usually received years after Baptism when it involves an infant, completes the baptismal process through a special invocation of the Holy Spirit and anointing with sacred oil.

> *Eucharist*, also called the Mass, is the daily and Sunday worship that is at the heart of all Catholic life. Every Catholic should worship every Sunday as the foundation of his or her life. (Elements of the Mass will be elaborated later.)

Two sacraments provide healing of body and/or of spirit.

> *Anointing of the Sick* happens when priests come to those who are seriously ill, prays over them,

imposes hands on them, and then touches their foreheads and hands with consecrated oil. This practice goes back to ancient biblical times.

Reconciliation, often called Confession, happens when a Catholic comes to a priest to acknowledge sin; the priest prays a solemn prayer of absolution over the penitent so she or he may accept the mercy and healing of God more deeply.

Two sacraments deal with fundamental Christian callings, that is, specific ways of living as a disciple.

Matrimony is the sacrament by which people consecrate themselves to each other in Jesus for a life of exclusive love, centered on family life. Catholics consider marriage to be a life-long, and exclusive, commitment.

Holy Orders refer to the levels of ordained service in the Catholic Church: deacon, priest, and bishop. Catholics consider each level of service to be a permanent state of commitment. Many people know Catholic sisters, or nuns. There is no sacrament to make someone a nun. Rather, Catholics consider this form of religious life as a way to intensify the basic calling that comes in baptism.

The Communion of Saints

Saints are holy people. They can be living or dead, but they have to be holy. Saint Paul in his letter to the

Ephesians instructs us to "equip the saints for the work of ministry." References are made to saints both living and dead.

The process of how a saint is named a saint is fascinating, but we won't have time to go into right now. It is not an easy thing to be named a saint. In fact the term "devil's advocate" came from the church appointed person who argued against a person being named the saint. You really have to prove a case for sainthood. Who knew?

We are surrounded by saints from our past and in our present who have proved to be solid gold when tested in the furnace of life's challenges. Saints are there to inspire us and to intercede for us. There's a patron saint for so many of our jobs, life situations, and causes. Some of them may seem a little strange at first. For instance, Saint Gerard, a man, is the patron saint of childbirth. Or Anthony is the patron saint of domestic animals. (Makes you wonder who the patron saint of imported animals is, doesn't it?) It seems singularly appropriate that the patron saint of bakers is Elizabeth of Hungary. Whenever you are "hungry" for some baked goods, think of Elizabeth.

It would seem that we have patron saints for everyone and everything. There are patrons for bankers and beggars, plasterers and poets, secretaries and steelworkers. Sometimes, patron saints appear to have conflicts of interest. For instance, Matthew is the patron saint for accountants as well as the patron saint of tax collectors. Two people on opposite sides of the desk could ask his intercessory powers at the same meeting. Wait until the IRS hears of this loophole!

Catholics have a few favorite saints...our "go to" people. When we lose our car keys, someone is likely to pray, "Saint Anthony, Saint Anthony come around. My keys are lost, and can't be found." Saint Jude is the patron saint of lost causes. We have patrons for persons with mental illness or cancer, sore throats and headaches. We ask these saints to intercede for us because they know what our plight is all about. We learn from their stories and are inspired by them. They, in turn, are interested in our stories and situations. We believe in a communion of saints made up of those saints, both living and dead.

Saints inspire us to live good, virtuous holy lives. We seek their intercession. Mary knew what it was like to be a parent, to lose her son, to watch her child be a victim of violence, to walk with God through difficult times, and to reach out to people when they were in need. Her prayer for us is powerful. We go to Mary, knowing that she has often experienced what we have experienced. We go to Mary knowing that a Mother's Love will be given to us. And, to be honest, we go to Mary knowing her son finds it hard to refuse her request. (Read the Gospel story of the Wedding Feast at Cana in John 2.)

Saints model holiness for us in difficult situations. They intercede for us through difficult situations. It doesn't get much better than that!

Basic Catholic Prayers

The heart of Catholic life is the Eucharist, and the Celebration of the Eucharist is normally referred to as the Mass, which we will look over below. Many, however, seem more puzzled by other Catholic devotions such as the Rosary, the Stations of the Cross, and Benediction of the Most Blessed Sacrament. Some words on these devotions will be helpful.

The Lord's Prayer (Our Father)

Our Father, who art in heaven, hallowed be thy name. Thy kingdom come, thy will be done on earth as it is in heaven. Give us this day our daily bread, and forgive us our trespasses as we forgive those who trespass against us. And lead us not into temptation, but deliver us from evil. Amen.

The Hail Mary

Hail Mary, full of grace, the Lord is with thee. Blessed art thou among women, and blessed is the fruit of thy womb, Jesus. Holy Mary, Mother of God, pray for us sinners, now and at the hour of our death. Amen.

Glory Be

Glory be to the Father, and to the Son, and to the Holy Spirit. As it was in the beginning, is now, and ever shall be, world without end. Amen.

Catholic Devotions

The Rosary

This prayer form evolved over many centuries; some trace it back to the early monks who went into the desert of Egypt after AD 250, some of whom used stones to count the number of their prayers. Slowly throughout the middle ages, the form of the Rosary which most Catholics use came into being.

The impetus for the Rosary came from monastic life where monks would sing the psalms throughout the day; they viewed these psalms as the very prayer of Christ, eternally prayed by him in heaven. Monks, through their chants, became one with Christ's unending prayer.

There are 150 psalms. Devout lay people wanted to imitate the monks but obviously could not because they had everyday tasks to do, tasks that were necessary for life and society. As a result, in place of the 150 psalms, people would say 150 prayers. These prayers varied over the centuries, but eventually took on the form they now have: a succession of ten prayers composed of the Hail Mary prayer, begun with the Our Father (Lord's Prayer), and concluded with the Glory Be. A full Rosary would consist of 150 Hail Mary prayers; most people pray 50 Hail Mary prayers as their practice of saying the Rosary.

These series of ten Hail Mary prayers (called a decade) are accompanied by meditations on "the mysteries," that is, events, or traditional images, from the life of Christ. Catholics who say the Rosary find a tremendous source of peace and insight. The repetition of the prayers becomes almost a mantra, and the scenes of Jesus and Mary challenge the one praying to deeper commitment.

The Stations of the Cross

In the Middle Ages, when the Holy Land became accessible to Christians during the time of the Crusades, devout and brave Christians would make the dangerous pilgrimage there, visiting those places traditionally associated with the final walk of Jesus to his death.

So many people wanted to do this, but were unable to for a variety of reasons, that there sprang up a devotional practice whereby the walk of Jesus became spiritually available to any Christian. Religious leaders, particularly the Franciscan friars, set up scenes from the final journey of Jesus to his death in parish churches or on outdoor paths; they called these scenes "stations" or stopping points. Eventually fourteen stations became the norm for Catholics.

Catholics particularly make the Stations during the season of Lent, the forty-day period before Easter, notably on Fridays. Many Catholic parishes feature the devotion of the Stations on Good Friday, when they remember the death of Jesus in a solemn way. Many people who are not Catholics find strength in this devotional practice.

Benediction

This practice involves the Eucharist (the consecrated Bread) that remains after people have received communion at Mass. As a sign of particular devotion to the presence of Jesus in this sacrament, Catholics would show the consecrated host in a conspicuous way in order to help deepen appreciation of Christ's presence in the Eucharist and intensify devotion to him.

Parishes celebrate this devotion at various times that differ quite a bit depending on the parish. In the simple ceremony of Benediction, the host is taken from the tabernacle (the box where it is kept after Mass), and placed in a vessel where it can be seen while Catholics solemnly kneel. Then the priest or deacon will use the vessel to make the Sign of the Cross over the people as a sign of Christ's blessing (that is, benediction) over the people. People say some final prayers and sing a closing hymn.

Children may celebrate Benediction at certain times of the year, particularly after Easter when we reflect on the Eucharist as God's special gift to the Church.

The Eucharist (Mass)

The Mass will seem bewildering to someone unfamiliar with it—like a string of unconnected events, like many details that might obscure the big picture. Once, however, someone has a big picture, then the various parts of the Mass fit into place.

If you remember the story of the two disciples walking to Emmaus (Luke 24:13ff.), it will help clarify the major parts of the Mass. In that story, the two disciples are leaving Jerusalem after Jesus' death, confused and despairing. Jesus joins them, though they do not recognize him in his risen state. As the three walk, Jesus first opens for them the meaning of the Scriptures (that is, the Jewish writings of the Old Testament). Then, after they have walked for a while, they stop for the evening at an inn. During the meal, Jesus breaks bread and gives it to them—at this moment, they recognize him. So Jesus first opens the meaning of the Scriptures, and then Jesus breaks bread with his disciples.

The Mass has two major parts which correspond with this story: in the first part, we read and explore the Word of God. In the second part, we focus on the table (the altar), thank God in Jesus, and then eat the food of Holy Communion. Two parts: Scripture and Table—or "The Liturgy of the Word," and the "Liturgy of the Eucharist." These structure the celebration of the Mass.

The First Part of the Mass: The Liturgy of the Word

In the first part of the Mass, the church reads three times from the Scripture. Two readings precede the reading from the Gospel. The **First Reading** usually comes from the Old Testament, the original Jewish Scriptures, followed by the singing or recitation of a **psalm**; the **Second Reading** usually comes from a letter from the early apostles, with St. Paul serving as the primary writer. Then the **Gospel** is read—the congregation stands for this because the Gospel is a form of Christ's presence with us. The priest or deacon then gives a talk (called a homily) to help the congregation reflect on the sacred readings. This part of the Mass usually takes about a half hour, but can vary depending on the practice of the local parish.

Everything else (the opening hymn, the singing or praying of the Gloria, the opening prayer (called "the Collect") either prepares for these readings or follows them up (the reciting of the Creed and the prayers of request which we call the Prayer of the Faithful).

If you are attending Mass, try to catch the drift of the readings; usually the first reading will find an echo in the Gospel. Catholics stand and sit at various times during the first part—just do what everyone else does, and it will begin to seem natural for you.

The Second Part of the Mass: The Liturgy of the Eucharist

The second part of the Mass involves three main actions. First, the congregation presents bread and wine as a sign of the gift of itself in love to God. Almost all parishes on Sunday will take up a collection at this part of the Mass. When the gifts are presented, this concludes with a prayer (Prayer over the Gifts).

Next the priest, on behalf of the people, gives God praise and thanksgiving in the most solemn way. The priest states the reason why we give thanks—God's generosity, or God's love, or God's salvation in Jesus, for example—and the congregation responds with words that come from the prophet Isaiah ("Holy, holy, holy"). The congregation then kneels for the part of the Mass when we call the Holy Spirit upon the gifts of bread and wine remember the night before Jesus died and how he said the blessing and gave the bread and wine as living memory of him, and pray for the world and the Church. This part ends with the powerful words of the priest giving glory to God: "Through him and with him and in him, O God, almighty Father, in the unity of the Holy Spirit, all glory and honor is yours, for ever and ever." The congregation affirms this prayer by singing or proclaiming loudly: Amen.

Finally comes the communion part of the Mass, when we prepare to receive the Body of Christ (the consecrated bread) and, very often, the Blood of Christ (the consecrated wine) in an extremely sacred part of the Mass which we call Holy Communion. Before we do this, we pray the Lord's Prayer, and exchange a Sign of Peace in the love of Christ. After we receive Communion, we spend some time in prayer which concludes with a formal prayer (Prayer after Communion).

The Mass ends with the priest or deacon sending the congregation forth in words which encourage them to live out their faith in the world. The priest makes a Sign of the Cross over the people in solemn blessings just before the closing hymn.

Try to keep these two main parts of the Mass in mind when you attend. Listen for the readings. Watch for the gifts of bread and wine, the solemn prayers, and the congregation going up to the altar for Communion. The more you participate and see the main outline, the more familiar the Mass—and its meaning—will become for you.

Points to Ponder

1. What if any questions remain for you regarding the church?

2. What do you think are some of the greatest misunderstandings of the Church that people have?

3. Are there any Catholic practices or devotions with which you would like to be more familiar? (The Rosary, or Novenas, or different prayers, fasting, outreach to the poor, etc)

4. Name something from your own spiritual tradition or faith journey that is meaningful to you. What makes this a significant part of your life? How has this tradition been passed on to you and how do you share it with others?